21st Century
Junior Library

DISCOVER THE
TRICERATOPS

Jennifer Zeiger

**Our Prehistoric World:
Dinosaurs**

Published in the United States of America by:

CHERRY LAKE PRESS
2395 South Huron Parkway, Suite 200, Ann Arbor, Michigan 48104
www.cherrylakepress.com

Content Adviser: Gregory M. Erickson, PhD, Dinosaur Paleontologist, Department of Biological
Science, Florida State University, Tallahassee, Florida

Reading Adviser: Marla Conn, ReadAbility, Inc.

Photo and Illustration Credits: Cover: © Orla/Shutterstock.com; pages 5, 11: © Herschel Hoffmeyer/
Shutterstock.com; page 6: © leonello calvetti/Shutterstock.com; page 7: © BY MOVIE/Shutterstock.com;
page 9: © Alberto Andrei Rosu/Shutterstock.com; page 10: © David Herraez Calzada/Shutterstock.com;
page 12: © Elina/Dreamstime.com; pages 13, 18: © Dotted Yeti/Shutterstock.com; page 14: © Mohamad
Haghani/Alamy; page 17: © Stocktrek Images, Inc./Alamy; page 20 left: © Wawritto/Dreamstime.com;
page 20 right: © Kumar Sriskandan/Alamy; page 21: © steve estvanik/Shutterstock.com

Cherry Lake Press is an imprint of Cherry Lake Publishing Group.

Library of Congress Cataloging-in-Publication Data has been filed and is available at catalog.loc.gov.

Cherry Lake Press would like to acknowledge the work of the Partnership for 21st Century Learning, a Network
of Battelle for Kids. Please visit http://www.battelleforkids.org/networks/p21 for more information.

Printed in the United States of America

Note from publisher: Websites change regularly, and their future contents are outside of our control.
Supervise children when conducting any recommended online searches for extended learning opportunities.

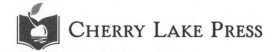

CHERRY LAKE PRESS

CONTENTS

WHAT WAS TRICERATOPS?

A huge dinosaur moves slowly through the marsh. It tears up a bunch of tasty ferns. The *Triceratops* raises its head as it chews. It watches for predators. Suddenly, a hungry *Tyrannosaurus rex* rushes across the marsh. The *Triceratops* has to defend itself. It is ready to fight with its sharp horns.

Tyrannosaurus rex may have been a common predator of *Triceratops*.

Triceratops lived 68 to 65 million years ago. It was found in North America. It was one of the last dinosaurs on Earth. All dinosaurs became **extinct** around 65 million years ago.

The word *triceratops* means "three-horned face."

Ask Questions!

How do scientists know when certain dinosaurs lived? If you don't know the answer, ask! A librarian or teacher can help you find the answer.

WHAT DID TRICERATOPS LOOK LIKE?

Triceratops was very big. An adult weighed more than an elephant does. It was almost as long as a small school bus. The dinosaur's four legs were very strong. This helped them carry the dinosaur's heavy body.

Triceratops needed strong, solid legs to move its 6-ton (5,400 kilogram) body.

Triceratops's head was huge. It was among the largest of any land animal ever. It took up one-third of the dinosaur's length. A **frill** stuck out from the back of *Triceratops*'s head. Two long horns were above its eyes. There was another horn on its snout. It was shorter than the others.

Triceratops's head could be about 10 feet (3 meters) long.

Triceratops's beak was quite sharp.

At the end of *Triceratops*'s snout was a beak. This beak curved down. This is much like a parrot's beak today. The dinosaur's mouth was full of teeth. These were behind the dinosaur's beak.

Look!

Take a close look at a picture of *Triceratops*. Does it look like any animals alive today? What animals have horns? Do any have frills on their heads? What kinds of animals have beaks?

13

A *Triceratops* had to protect itself and its territory.

HOW DID TRICERATOPS LIVE?

Scientists believe *Triceratops* lived alone. It needed to protect its territory. It also had to defend itself. Its horns helped it battle other *Triceratops*. Scientists found frills that might have been damaged by other *Triceratops* horns. The dinosaurs may have fought over territory or a mate.

No one is sure why *Triceratops* had a frill. It might have helped protect the dinosaur's neck from attackers.

The frill might also have been for show. The dinosaurs may have known one another by their frills. The frill may also have helped them find a mate.

Create!

Scientists do not know how *Triceratops*'s frill was colored. What color do you guess it was? Draw a picture of a *Triceratops*. Color your drawing with crayons or colored pencils.

Triceratops's frill might have been very colorful.

Triceratops was an herbivore, or plant eater.

Plants made up *Triceratops*'s diet. The dinosaur mostly ate ferns and other low-growing plants. These plants could be very tough. *Triceratops* cut bites off of them with its sharp beak. Its back teeth were like scissors. They were used to slice up food.

We know about *Triceratops* through its fossils. These fossils have been found in the United States and Canada. The most complete *Triceratops* skeleton yet is on display in the Melbourne Museum in Australia. It is 85% complete. Do you want to study dinosaurs? Maybe you will make a big *Triceratops* discovery!

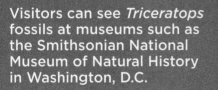

Visitors can see *Triceratops* fossils at museums such as the Smithsonian National Museum of Natural History in Washington, D.C.

GLOSSARY

diet (DYE-it) the food an animal typically eats

extinct (ik-STINGKT) describing a type of plant or animal that has completely died out

fossils (FAH-suhlz) the preserved remains of living things from thousands or millions of years ago

frill (FRILL) a structure made of bone, feathers, or fur sticking out over the neck of an animal

marsh (MAHRSH) an area of wet, muddy land

mate (MATE) the male or female partner of a pair of animals

predators (PRED-uh-turz) animals that live by hunting other animals for food

skeleton (SKEL-uh-tuhn) the framework of bones that supports and protects the body of an animal

territory (TER-uh-tor-ee) an area of land claimed by an animal

FIND OUT MORE

Books

Braun, Dieter. *Dictionary of Dinosaurs: An Illustrated A to Z of Every Dinosaur Ever Discovered.* New York, NY: Chartwell Books, 2022.

Mara, Wil. *Triceratops.* New York, NY: Children's Press, 2012.

Rockwood, Leigh. *Triceratops.* New York, NY: PowerKids Press, 2012.

Websites

With an adult, learn more online with these suggested searches.

Britannica Kids—Triceratops
Check out *Triceratops* and other ancient animals.

National Geographic Kids—Triceratops
Learn more cool facts about *Triceratops*.

INDEX

ABOUT THE AUTHOR

Jennifer Zeiger lives in Chicago, Illinois. She writes and edits children's books on all sorts of topics.